T0151244

THE MONUMENT

ALSO BY COLLEEN WAGNER:

down from heaven
Eclipsed
Home
The Living
The Morning Bird
Sand

THE MONUMENT
COLLEEN WAGNER

PLAYWRIGHTS CANADA PRESS
TORONTO

The Monument © copyright 1996 Colleen Wagner

For professional or amateur production rights, please contact:
Michael Petrasek, Kensington Literary
34 St. Andrew Street, Toronto, ON M5T 1K6
416.848.9648, kensingtonlit@rogers.com

LIBRARY AND ARCHIVES CANADA CATALOGUING IN PUBLICATION
Wagner, Colleen
The monument / Colleen Wagner. -- 2nd ed.

Play.
Also available in electronic format.
ISBN 978-0-88754-944-1

I. Title.

PS8626.U7512M65 2010   C812'.6   C2010-905838-0

Playwrights Canada Press acknowledges that we operate on land, which, for
thousands of years, has been the traditional territories of the Mississaugas
of the New Credit, the Huron-Wendat, the Anishinaabe, Métis, and the
Haudenosaunee peoples. Today, this meeting place is home to many
Indigenous peoples from across Turtle Island and we are grateful to have
the opportunity to work and play here.

We acknowledge the financial support of the Canada Council for the
Arts—which last year invested $153 million to bring the arts to Canadians
throughout the country—the Ontario Arts Council (OAC), the Ontario
Media Development Corporation, and the Government of Canada for our
publishing activities.

In memory of my mother,
Lucille Anne Wagner (née Caskey)

Canada's reputation, at least until recently, has been that of a peacemaking country, a nation that takes great pride in its soldiers observing, witnessing, and maintaining the peace in wartorn countries. The work of our armed forces as peacekeepers in the former country of Yugoslavia contributed to what I consider an ethic as well as a politic of peace, law, and order. When I think of the best of Canada's role in the world, I think of this. I think of the memorial in Ottawa, three soldiers—two men and one woman—watching, listening, and witnessing.

In 1992, Colleen returned to Canada after travelling for thirteen months in Southeast Asia. She had witnessed civil unrest in almost every country, countered by brutal suppression by military governments. Once again having access to a newspaper in English, she was affected by a photograph of a Somali man, barbed wire around his neck, being dragged across the street. That year forty-three civil wars were raging. The Quakers were in Yugoslavia during the genocide as social witnesses and she was receiving diskettes—stories of people living through this horror, many of whom were women who spoke not just of genocide but of systematic rape, the intentional impregnating of women with "enemy" children, and sexual slavery. Colleen began to write the opening monologue of The Monument.

My experience of this play began before I knew of it. I read an article about the arrest of a young Yugoslavian militiaman of Serbian heritage for war crimes, specifically the rape and murder of a number of women, mainly Muslim women of Bosnian heritage. Their bodies were found in a mass grave. A concentration camp was also discovered. I recall my own reaction to this story in the newspapers and the picture of the young militiaman. His picture in the paper made him look monstrous. His crime was monstrous. His age was much too young. Can human beings actually do this to each other? What kind of sexual behaviour or motivation or inclination makes such serial crimes possible? How did this young soldier live with himself? The mind is stunned by the darkness of the thoughts necessary to commit such a crime repeatedly. Then I received Colleen's first draft. In it was anger and determination to give order to the emotional chaos of this story from the Yugoslavian civil war and the forty-two other wars that year and all wars since time immemorial.

The ancient military tactic of rape as a weapon of war had resurfaced and suddenly what had seemed to have been forgotten or filed as historical was everywhere. In the Yugoslavian civil war, soldiers were jacked up with drugs, liquor, and porn to motivate them to rape the other side's women. This tactic was not only intended to violate the women, marking their psyches and sexuality for life but also to ensure these women would be rejected by their husbands and families after hostilities had ceased. Better if they were impregnated. Eros was to be murdered—the survival instinct, propagation of the community, sex, and other creative life-producing drives were poisoned by this tactic. What contemporary military commander could think of this as an instrument of war? This was one of the questions that arose in talkbacks for this show, when it was first produced in the mid-1990s. To "rape and pillage" was from another time, and like many audience members I was surprised at the calculation of Yugoslavian generals in employing this technique in the twentieth century. Somehow in this particular war, the world had returned to an ancient barbarism. Only in 1998 did Louise Arbour convince the United Nations that rape was a war crime. In 2010, rape, although illegal, continues to be part of military conflict—the Congo and Darfur are only two present-day testaments.

When I began working on *The Monument*, I talked to my father, a veteran of the Second World War, about this play and the current Yugoslavian war. We both had travelled Yugoslavia, me first when I hitchhiked through Tito's communist state in the mid-'70s, then the two of us together when I toured a show in the mid-'80s to the BITEF Festival. Even then, the artists we talked to felt that the rotating presidency from each nationality was faltering and feared Slobodan Milosevic's rabble-rousing Serbian nationalist rhetoric at soccer games. My father told me a story he had heard from one of his clients, who had left Yugoslavia after the Second World War. She said that despite the length and harshness of Tito's iron rule uniting the nationalities of his manufactured country, the desire for vengeance was buried but not dead. She said that during that Second World War, a young Serbian man and a young Croatian woman had fallen in love, their respective communities separated only by the Sava River. One side or the other kidnapped the couple, stripped the skin off them, tied their bodies together as if in copulation, strapped them to a pole on a raft, and floated them down the river. In fifty years, she said, nothing had changed. Vengeance for acts like these was only waiting for its opportunity. This was a deep-rooted revenge, historically continuous, buried but not dead—a horror repetitive and endless. How to make sense of this? How to end this ongoing cycle? How to prevent such horrific crimes? These are the questions that Colleen addresses in her play.

The Monument's two characters, Stetko and Mejra, embark on a dramatic journey that becomes as horrific as Stetko's original crime. Saving Stetko from the electric chair, Mejra, as his guardian, inevitably becomes complicit in his world of endless violence. The play's events are simple—the act of eating, the plowing of the land, the care of a wounded animal, the nurturing of a budding plant in war-scorched soil—simple but essential tasks as Mejra attempts to break Stetko's defiance and will. They are the tasks of survival. After the war food must be grown, life must be sustained. But life cannot go on. Nothing is normal. Every day is marked by their war experiences. The simple, the normal, the life-sustaining are all compromised by inexpressible remorse or paralyzing anger. Mejra's desire to get Stetko to reveal the unmarked grave of her daughter involves brutal punishment, slave labour, and psychological torture motivated by her justifiable outrage. The only way to get him to experience empathy is to torture him with the thought of losing his girlfriend the same way Mejra is tortured by the loss of her daughter. Guardian and criminal switch the roles of perpetrator and victim. It is a credit to Colleen that she makes it impossible to judge either of them.

In the dramaturgical development of the play, there was passionate discussion (always a sign of a good play) about what happens after the monument is built. Should Mejra just kill Stetko? What does she do with her unending grief, her bottomless rage, the impossibility of closure? How can Stetko return to any semblance of normalcy? What does he do with the indelible stain on his soul, his life of shame and guilt, his ever-present death drive? There could be no forgiveness for the crime of mass murder and rape — Stetko's crime was against humanity. If Mejra does not kill Stetko, can closure be possible for either character, or for the story itself? Steko can't leave, he can only ask for Mejra's forgiveness. Mejra's impulse to forgive can only be unconscious because if she thinks about it, she will have to kill him. Ultimately, Colleen leaves the characters at the fulcrum of change and the audience at the tipping point of judgment.

The building of the monument of corpses on stage, which concludes with Stetko's confession, is a remarkable event. In our world where we see so many monuments to warriors and commanders through all time — I think of the relentlessness of those sculptural images, particularly when I am in London, England, or in Washington or in Ottawa (during the Second World War, my father, the young officer, would hang around the World War One monument after work). I ask myself, why is all this bronze and art devoted solely to warriors? It seems that only since the Holocaust have the victims of war become part of what must always be remembered. Mejra's monument not only remembers the victims but viscerally demonstrates the consequences of war.

It may be a way "art"—this rotting sculpture—can evince the feelings and thoughts that might prevent the next war. Mejra's monument of the real victims' rotting flesh and whitening skeletons brings horror home into our consciousness. Ironically, the impulse to revenge is unearthed and brought into the public eye for all to see. It is externalized and put on display as a motivation for revenge. The lives of those women and their legacies to the living are not to be forgotten. The desire for revenge is not to be buried for use in the next war but recognized publicly to prevent it.

Colleen Wagner's *The Monument* has been produced around the world. What has struck me about the play's production history is how many times it has been presented in countries that have recently experienced civil war or war between states, or have seemed on the edge of war or engaged in cold war. It has been performed in Taiwan, in mainland China, in Romania and Rwanda. This is another kind of testament, that countries that know the trauma of recent war want to talk about war. Revenge is still fresh for them.

Recently, I read a Rwandan story of how that country and its people have put into action the act of reconciliation. A man who murdered a woman's family (in front of her) must every morning pick her up from her home and drive her to work and then pick her up and drive her home again at the end of the day. He is tasked with the responsibility of protecting her and serving her in this way. At each day's beginning and its end, they must face each other and engage each other simply as human beings. The task is formidable but it is simple, and while the courage required for it seems unimaginable, it engages the instinct to survive. This is what Colleen Wagner, playwright and peacekeeper, is asking us to do in *The Monument*.

—Richard Rose
Artistic Director, Tarragon Theatre

The Monument premiered in January 1995 at the Canadian Stage Company, Toronto, in co-production with Necessary Angel Theatre and the Manitoba Theatre Centre. It was produced in Manitoba in February 1995 with the same cast:

MEJRA   Rosemary Dunsmore
STATKO   Tom Barnett

Directed by Richard Rose
Set and costumes by Charlotte Dean
Lighting by Kevin Lamotte
Stage managed by Naomi Campbell

A second performance was presented at Northern Light Theatre, Edmonton, Alberta, April 1995 with the following cast:

MEJRA   Maralyn Ryan
STETKO   Kurt Max Runte

Directed by DD Kugler
Set and costumes by David Skelton
Lighting by Stancil Campbell
Sound design by Dave Clarke
Stage managed by Susan Hayes

The play was performed at La Mama, Melbourne, Australia, July 1995 with the following cast:

MEJRA	Brenda Palmer
STETKO	Bob Pavlich

Directed by Laurence Strangio
Set and costumes by Anna Tregloan
Lighting by Richard Vabre
Stage managed by Jeni Hector

I against my brother
I and my brother against our cousin
I, my brother, and cousin against the neighbour
All of us against the foreigner
          —Bedouin proverb

A voice was heard in Ramah,
Sobbing and lamenting
Rachel weeping for her children,
refusing to be comforted
because they were no more.
          —Jeremiah 31:15

CHARACTERS

STETKO, nineteen
MEJRA, fifty

SCENE 1

STETKO is strapped to an electric chair. A single bulb above him provides the only light. He appears small in the vast darkness. He speaks to spectators sitting in a gallery behind or around him. We cannot see the gallery or the spectators.

STETKO   The one I liked the best was seventeen, maybe eighteen.
And pretty. With watery eyes.
Like a doe's.
She was like that.

I was her first.
I mean, she was a virgin.

A man can tell.
She said she wasn't, but the way she bled—
and cried—
I knew.

I didn't mean to hurt her.
Every time she cried out I pulled back.
I wanted it to last.

    Pause.

I don't care for orgasm like some men.
They only think about coming. They rush through
like they're pumping iron,
just wanting to come.
Not me.
Once you come that's it.
It's over.
And there you are facing the same old things that
were there before you started.

I don't care for the world much.

(laughs) 'Course it doesn't care much for me either.
So big deal, eh?
It don't care for me, I don't care for it…
Big deal.

The doctors—make me laugh—they're trying to
figure me out.
Why I'm like this.
Nobody agrees.
Dr. Casanova— Yeah! Casanova! I think he's joking
when he tells me his name. I laugh in his face.
He stares back.

He's got eyes like a chicken's.
Beady.
And small.
So I don't say nothing.
We have 106 sessions and I don't say anything. Not a word. We stare at each other for one hour, 106 times.
He thinks I'm a "passive aggressive."
I think he's fucking nuts.

They bring in another doctor.
A woman.
She comes with a bodyguard.
'Cause I'm dangerous.
That's what the bodyguard said.
"Dangerous."
I say to her, "Wanna fuck?"
She says, "And then go to the forest?"
I know what she's doing—egging me on.
Trying to trick me.
Get me to talk.
I look at her and I think, this doctor has never done it except in a nice soft bed and she doesn't do it much, and she doesn't like it when she does do it.
She's got a tight puckered mouth.
I said to her: "Is your ass like your mouth?"
She says, "No. One exhales, the other inhales. Don't yours?"
She's funny. So I talk to her.
Except,
I don't tell her where the bodies are.

I don't remember.

   Pause.

I tell her about my girlfriend.
My girlfriend's a virgin.
She wants to do it but there's no place.
She lives at home.
Whenever we'd go into her room her mother would listen at the door and open it all of a sudden and poke her head in. "It's too quiet in here," she'd say. "If you got nothing to say then you can join us in the living room. If you do have something to say, say it and come out here. It's not good for people to spend too much time alone together when they've got nothing to say." She should talk. I don't think she's said two words to her husband since "I do" at the wedding.

We couldn't do it at my place 'cause I was in the army. Some men would bring their girlfriends to the camp and would do it while others watched.
I can't come when people are watching. And the men never let you forget it when you don't come.
So I never brought my girlfriend.

I never took her to the forest.

I think she's watching.
I don't want her to think I'm nervous.
I didn't eat or drink since yesterday.
I don't want to mess my pants in front of her.

After I was arrested she went to the camps where the women were held.
They told her that I'd been there and raped twenty-three girls.
At first I told her it wasn't true.
It wasn't really.
I mean I had to.

The other men forced me.
First time I said no they stripped me naked and laughed at me—said I had no dick, said I turned into a girl all of a sudden, that maybe they should do it to me.

So I did it.

I couldn't come.
So they rubbed my face in shit and made me do it till I came.

I faked it.

She just laid there looking at me.
She didn't care. She gave up.
She didn't even blink when I was doing it to her.
Just laid there like she was dead.

After it was over they told me to kill her.
I had to. I had lowest rank.
We took her to the forest and I shot her with my machine gun and hid her body under a log. It'd been raining and she was covered in mud. Somebody might have mistaken her for a dead pig.

That was the first time I did it.
Sex.

I didn't mind killing her 'cause she knew I faked it and I didn't want her telling anyone.
It was like that.

We went to the prison camps about every three days after that and would pick out women and we'd all do it then drive them out to the forest. We'd rape them again then kill them.

Everybody was doing it.
I don't know why.

That's where I saw the one I liked.
In one of the camps.
I was the first.

I got nothing against those "people" personally.
I was seventeen.
I had to enlist. If I didn't they'd think I was a sympathizer and they'd kill my family.
Only soldiers were getting paid.
My brothers and I were the only ones in the family making any money.
I drove a cab before, but with the war nobody was taking them. Besides, only the army could buy gas.

So you do what comes up.

Who knows what that will be, eh—what life brings?
You're born.
You die.
And in between you try to live a little.

Maybe it's fate, eh?—our lives.

Pause.

I'm not proud of what I did and I'm sorry my girlfriend found out.
I'm sorry we couldn't do it before I die.

Pause.

I did to the one I liked what I wanted to do to my girlfriend because I knew my girlfriend wouldn't let me do it to her.

It was getting harder and harder to get it up.
I knew one day I'd get caught faking it.
So I took this girl to the forest after we raped her.
I got to drive alone.
The others thought I was taking her there to kill her.
I tied her up to a tree so she was just off the ground and started talking to her.
I told her about my girlfriend, about me driving cab, and about my uncle, who has a still out back of his house, and how he's always dodging the authorities and selling to them at the same time. I tell her she's pretty,
that she reminds me of my girlfriend.
My girlfriend's studying to be a nurse.
She says she wants to put some good back into the world.

I would too.
If I knew how.
Who wouldn't, eh?
If they knew how.

Pause.

So I take all her clothes off and she's crying and begging me not to do it.
I want to
but I don't.

Her crying doesn't stop me.
I can't get it up.
I can't do it anymore.

That's what I really regret.
That I didn't do it with my girlfriend before I got caught. I think I could have come with her.

The woman doctor, Nika, Dr. Nika—she wouldn't tell me her first name—said that was reserved for friends. Obviously I wasn't one of them.
I don't know what she told the authorities, but next thing you know I'm being tried for war crimes.
Makes me laugh.
If war is a crime why do we keep having them?
Why isn't everybody arrested?
They show us porno films and tell us doing it to women is good for morale and they bring women in and then after the war is over they tell us what we did is a crime.
After it's over you find out there were rules.
Like no raping women.
(ironic) No massacres.
Just good clean fighting—as if it were a duel, as if it were honourable.
As if you were brave.

Men aren't brave. We're all so scared we're going to die we do anything to stay alive. We'll shoot a guy in the back. We'll creep into his bedroom in the middle of the night and shoot him in his sleep.

And we'll rape his wife and daughters.
Nobody's going to stop you.

Some of the men said we shouldn't kill the women.
We should get them all pregnant with our babies
and that's how we'd win the war.
Create a new race.

I heard some men were keeping women till after
they got them pregnant. Seven, eight months. Too
late for them to do anything about it.

It's a very good way to wipe out a race. Take away
their women and get them pregnant. Their own
husbands don't even want them after that. And
what's she going to do, kill her own baby and be
completely alone?

They're doing it to our women too!

I never did that.

I don't care who wins the war.
It was just a job.

I guess rape is just part of it.

> MEJRA *enters. She's dressed in black and stands
> to* STETKO's *right, which makes it difficult for him
> to see her. She looks at him impassively.*

> *Long, long silence.*

Are you the executioner?

> *No response.*

I guess it's only fitting that a woman do it.

Silence.

Women can't rape men.
Too bad, eh?
There's probably a lot of women who would if they
could.

Silence.

I'm as ready as I'll ever be.
I guess.

I suppose going for a piss before we begin is out of
the question.

He laughs. She remains silent.

I'm not going to say I'm sorry if that's what you're
waiting for.
What difference would it make?
It won't bring them back.
It won't undo what I did.
It won't make me a better man.

MEJRA   Won't it?

STETKO   Ah, she has a tongue.

Pause. He strains to see her.

(derisive) I'm sorry.
Feel better?

MEJRA   Should I?

STETKO   Isn't that what forgiveness is all about?
           I say sorry and the world forgives me.

           I'M SORRY.

               Silence.

           I don't mean it, of course, and so how can I expect
           forgiveness.

MEJRA   Is that what you want?

STETKO   I want to do it with my girlfriend.
           And I want to take a leak.
           My life is simple.

MEJRA   So take a leak.

           Do you think we haven't seen a man pee his pants
           before?

           If you were a dog you could pee down your leg quite
           easily.
           But you're not a dog, are you? And so you can't pee
           your own pants.
           You're too dignified for that.
           You may think other people act like animals, but
           not you. You're a good person.
           A good dog, who has only had a bad owner.

STETKO   Are you a doctor?

MEJRA   No.

STETKO   Missionary?

MEJRA   No.

STETKO   A mother?

MEJRA   …no.

          Silence.

STETKO   And you're not the executioner…?

MEJRA   I'm your saviour.

STETKO   Oh yeah?

MEJRA   Yes.

STETKO   Maybe I don't want to be saved.

MEJRA   That's up to you.

STETKO   What do you mean?

MEJRA   I can have you released.

STETKO   Is this a joke?

MEJRA   No joke.

STETKO   You can set me free?!

MEJRA   On condition.

STETKO   What condition?

MEJRA   You must do as I say for the rest of your life.

STETKO	Do as—just do whatever you say?
MEJRA	Yes.
STETKO	Like… anything?
MEJRA	Everything.
STETKO	No deal.
MEJRA	As you wish. *(begins to exit)*
STETKO	Wait! What if you asked me to kill myself?
MEJRA	Then you would have to do it.

Silence.

STETKO	Would you? Is that it? The state's too bankrupt to do it? It's a new way to save money—get the prisoners to do it themselves. That's it, isn't it? They're too cheap. Maybe the power's been cut off, eh. What a laugh!

Silence.

MEJRA	It's up to you.
STETKO	What kind of choice is that?
MEJRA	The only one you have.

STETKO   One choice is no choice.

MEJRA   You have two.

STETKO   I do it or they do it.

MEJRA   They do it or you obey me for the rest of your life.

           Silence.

STETKO   Why would they do that?

MEJRA   If you want to find out you'll have to postpone your
           death.

STETKO   What if I don't do as you tell me?

MEJRA   What do you think—that you'll get away with it?
           Run and hide
           —like a frightened dog?

           Where can you go?
           Everyone knows your face.

           You're the most hated man in the world.

STETKO   Is that true?

MEJRA   What do you think?
           You kill twenty-three young girls and people will
           love you for it?

STETKO   So why do you want to save me?

MEJRA	You'll have to agree to the conditions if you want to find out.
	(checking her watch) It's time.
	STETKO experiences a few frantic moments. MEJRA begins to leave.
STETKO	Sure! Okay. What have I got to lose.
	Lights out.

SCENE 2

That night. STETKO fingers the last morsels of food from a bowl and sucks his fingers clean.

STETKO	*(after a satisfying burp)* Very good. Prison food is the worst. Sometimes I wouldn't eat it. I left some in a corner once. Even the rats wouldn't touch it. But today I might have.
MEJRA	Freedom makes everything look good?
STETKO	Even makes you and your scowling face look good. So, you live here?

MEJRA	Yes.
STETKO	No husband about?
MEJRA	Killed.
STETKO	I lost a brother. And sister. Do you have any beer?
MEJRA	Yes, but none of it is for you.
STETKO	Aah. I see.
MEJRA	What do you see?
STETKO	Nothing.
MEJRA	Then why do you say "I see" when you in fact see nothing?
STETKO	It's just a phrase.
MEJRA	It's also a lie.
STETKO	Truth. Lie. What difference does it make?
MEJRA	Don't you know?

Pause.

STETKO	What do you want me to say?
MEJRA	Tell the truth.

STETKO   Everybody said what I did was wrong. That I should die for what I did. Bad people are punished. Isn't that the truth? Bad people go to jail.
Good people, innocent people go free.
I'm free.
So tell me, am I bad or good?
What's the truth?

MEJRA   You're not free.

STETKO   From my shoes, things look different.

> MEJRA *swiftly picks up a small farm sickle that has been stuck in the ground, and with a single smooth motion deliberately slices off his ear. As he falls to the ground she clamps a collar and chain around his neck and fastens it to a bolt in the ground. He gasps for air.*

MEJRA   Get up.

> *She kicks him sharply. He cries and gasps on the ground.*

Get up!

> *He rises slowly, realizing as he rises that he is bound.*

STETKO   What is this—?!

> *She strikes him across the face and chest.*

What are you doing!?

> *She slaps his mouth.*

MEJRA   *(ordering)* You will be silent.

STETKO   Why are you doing this?

> *She strikes his mouth again.*

MEJRA   You will be silent.

> STETKO *goes to speak but thinks better of it.*
>
> MEJRA *begins to beat him, methodically, dispassionately, one open-handed slap after another.*
>
> STETKO *rages, straining to fight back.*

STETKO   STOP IT!

> *She stops.*

MEJRA   You will be silent and you will take your beating like a man.

STETKO   Why should I?

MEJRA   Because that's the deal.

STETKO   Are you going to beat me to death?

MEJRA   I am going to beat you until you fall to the ground or until I'm unable to beat you any longer.

> *She strikes him and* STETKO *immediately falls.*

Get up.

STETKO   I've fallen.

MEJRA   Get up you coward.

              Pause.

Last time.

              STETKO reluctantly but obediently rises.

Stand up tall.

              He leans into the collar and prepares himself for the beating. MEJRA *stands in front of him and begins the beating, a beating that seems to last forever.*

              The lighting changes to indicate a passing of time into night and a slivered moon. In this light we only see her back and her arms swinging back and forth as she strikes him.

              MEJRA *stops for a breath.*

Get down.

              He goes to his knees, shakily. She takes off a scarf and bandages his ear. They both fight back tears.

STETKO   Why did you do that?

MEJRA   Because you don't know the difference between the truth and a lie.

STETKO   I don't even know you.
          Do I?
          Have we ever met?
          Have I—have I ever done anything to you?

MEJRA   You don't know me.
          We've never met before.
          (finishing the bandaging) Not like a nurse would do
          it, not like your girlfriend, but it will serve its purpose.

STETKO   Do you know my girlfriend?

MEJRA   I know of her.

STETKO   Because of me?

MEJRA   Of course.

STETKO   She was there, wasn't she?
          At the jail?
          She must know I'm here.
          I'd like to see her.
          ...can I?

MEJRA   She's dead.

          Silence.

STETKO   I know she was there.

MEJRA   You saw her?

STETKO   She said she'd come.
          She said she'd see if she could come in with me—
          near the end.

MEJRA	She was shot on her way to the jail.
STETKO	*(on his feet)* You're lying!
MEJRA	If that's what you choose to believe.
STETKO	Tell me you're lying!
MEJRA	I'm lying.

Silence.

STETKO	Is it true?
MEJRA	Don't you know?
STETKO	*(stunned)* Is she really dead?
MEJRA	You tell me.
STETKO	Show me proof! The police report!
MEJRA	Why should I? Why should I tell you, prove to *you*? Who are you to ask for anything?
STETKO	I have a right to know the truth!

Long silence.

She's alive.
I know it.
You're playing games with my mind.
I know about mind games.

MEJRA   Time for bed.
            You sleep out here.

STETKO   Outside?

MEJRA   Outside.

            She exits. He stands stubbornly.

STETKO   Fuck you.
            Fuck you.

            Blackout.

SCENE 3

*STETKO, shackled, is yoked to a wooden plough.
MEJRA is behind, guiding it. The plow is stuck.*

MEJRA   Can't you pull harder, Stinko?

STETKO   It's Stetko.
            Stet-ko.

MEJRA   I prefer Stinko.

STETKO   I prefer not to pull harder.

MEJRA   You have no say in the matter.

            Silence.

            He leans into the yoke.

STETKO   It won't budge.

MEJRA   If we can't make something of this land we'll starve.

              They look at the charred ruins of the land.

STETKO   Sometimes I think we should all starve.
              We'd be better off.

MEJRA   *(laughing)* Stinko, you are so stupid you're funny.

STETKO   Don't call me Stinko, okay?
              Please.

              Pause.

MEJRA   Okay.

              Silence.

              He tries again. It won't budge.

STETKO   Maybe nothing will grow anyway.
              It's probably been poisoned.
              We sometimes sprayed.

MEJRA   There are land mines also.

STETKO   Here?!

MEJRA   Afraid to die?

STETKO   Everybody is afraid to die.

MEJRA   Is that so?

STETKO	Sure.
	Except when living looks worse. Then they want to die.
MEJRA	Were the women you killed like that?
STETKO	Some.
MEJRA	All?
STETKO	Some.
MEJRA	Who?
STETKO	I don't remember.
MEJRA	What were their names?
STETKO	I don't know.
	Why?

Silence.

MEJRA	Pull.
STETKO	It won't budge.
MEJRA	We have to dig it out.
STETKO	*(in the yoke)* How can I?

Long silence.

STETKO *grins.* MEJRA *begins to dig with her hands.* STETKO *leans against the plough and whistles a light tune.* MEJRA, *angry, digs harder, faster.*

(looking up) Sunstroke weather.

She looks up at him in anger. He grins back.

Take off the yoke, Mejra.

She resumes digging.

I've met people like you before.
Stubborn.
So stubborn they don't know when they're beat.
When they need the help of others. Even if they
don't like those others.

MEJRA   This rock was never here before!

STETKO   Maybe it's not a rock.
             Maybe it is a land mine.

             MEJRA *weeps.*

Hey, it's a joke.
It's a rock.

It's obvious it's a rock. I'm joking.

You have to laugh at life sometimes.
Otherwise you go mad.

MEJRA   That's your remedy, is it?

STETKO   *(shrugs)* Got a better idea?

> MEJRA *swiftly unhooks him from the yoke, cuffs his hands in front, and drags him by his chains to the rock.*

MEJRA   Dig it out.

STETKO   How?

MEJRA   With your feet. Your mouth. Your nose.
I don't care.
Just do it.

> STETKO *assesses the rock for a moment then proceeds to poke with one foot. He whistles a long note.*

STETKO   She's a big one.

MEJRA   Dig.

> *He works harder, using both feet. This motion develops into a kind of Russian jig or march. He sings and kicks at the dirt until he tires.*

STETKO   This is sunstroke weather.

MEJRA   For idiots, yes.

STETKO   What's life, eh?
Drudgery, and a few dances in between.
Care to dance, madam?

MEJRA   Dig.

STETKO   Take off my shirt.

It's hot.

I like the sun.
I never saw daylight in prison.
It's the first hot day of the year.

MEJRA *strikes him*

MEJRA   Stinko, you are nothing.
No one.
A dog.
A slave.
A murderer.

STETKO   I know what I am.
I know I'm a murderer
and a dog
and a slave.
I don't care.
I'm not proud.
I can be those things.

MEJRA   You *are* those things.

STETKO   So what?
So what do we do with that?
Kill me?
You went to a lot of trouble to save me.
Why? Eh?
What do you want?
I'm your dog and slave.
I'm Stinko the murderer.
So what?

She sits on the rock.

MEJRA	So what.
	Right.
	So what.
	What do we do with dogs and slaves and murderers.
	What would you do?
STETKO	Shoot them probably.
MEJRA	Shoot them.
STETKO	Yeah.
	It's simple.
MEJRA	Maybe I should shoot you.
STETKO	You like me.
MEJRA	Understand one thing if you can, stupido—I despise you.
STETKO	So shoot me.

Silence.

So use me like a dog and a slave till it's time to shoot me.
Do you think I care. Eh?
What do I have to care about?

MEJRA   Don't look for pity!
Dig!

Pause.

>He begins, furious at first, then grins and switches again to his manic dance, singing at the top of his lungs, kicking dirt everywhere until the rock is exposed. He clasps his handcuffed arms around the boulder and heaves with all his might and lifts the rock triumphantly to his chest. He turns as if he would hurl the rock at her, but it's impossible.

Go ahead.
Show me what you're really made of.
Smash my face with it.

>STETKO *laughs at his own impotence.*

Drop it on your foot.

STETKO   (*suddenly serious*) I can't.

MEJRA   Why not?

STETKO   I don't know.

>MEJRA *puts her foot beneath the rock.*

MEJRA   Drop it on mine.

>He releases the rock immediately. She pulls her foot away in time.

Try again.

STETKO   (*laughs*) It's too heavy.

MEJRA   Pick it up.

STETKO   You are one strange woman.

MEJRA   Who are you to judge?
              Pick it up.

              STETKO attempts to pick it up but can't.

STETKO   Impossible.

MEJRA   A moment ago it was possible.
              Pick it up or I'll bury you in this field.

STETKO   I can't pick it up now.
              I had strength then.
              I don't now.
              I used it all up.
              Who do you think I am—Hercules? I can lift moun-
              tains on command?

MEJRA   Didn't you kill on command?

              No response.

              Which is harder? Killing someone or lifting a
              mountain?
              Is that where your strength is, Stinko?
              In hatred?
              If you hate enough you can lift a mountain and kill
              a people, on command.

STETKO   I don't hate them.

MEJRA   You kill people you like?

              Silence.

Learn to hate me, Stinko, because you are going to lift that rock on command or be buried alive in this field.

STETKO   I wish you'd never come to save me.

MEJRA   I never came to save you.

STETKO   You said you were my savior.

MEJRA   I lied.

You know all about lies, don't you?
Haven't you ever said to a young girl, I'll show you the forest.

STETKO   I never!

MEJRA   Someday you'll take me to this forest.

STETKO   What do you mean?

MEJRA   You look nervous.
We all know about the forest.
Dead bodies.
Not your girlfriend though.
She died on the street.
A virgin.

STETKO weeps.

You're right, Stetko.
I am your savior.

Now pick up that rock because you owe me.

Pick it up out of gratitude instead of hate.

Go on.

He tries, but in vain.

Hate works best for you.

STETKO For you too.
You hate me.

MEJRA Yes.

STETKO Why?

MEJRA I might kill you before I could finish my sentence.

Pause.

STETKO You're one of "them," aren't you?

MEJRA What if I am?

STETKO My aunt is one.
My father's brother married one.
I used to see them a lot.
Before.

Now everybody fights.
The whole family.

Everyone thinks they're right.
That's why people need someone to take charge.
Keep people in line. Make them shut up and do as
they're told.

MEJRA   You?

STETKO   Not me,
               but somebody.

MEJRA   Then you'll like our arrangement.
               It's a dictatorship.
               I'm the dictator.
               I tell you what to do and you do it.

STETKO   Sure.
               I don't care.
               People don't care who's in charge just so long as
               they don't have to take responsibility.

MEJRA   I'll take responsibility.
               Pick up the rock and drop it on your foot.

STETKO   It's not normal to injure yourself.

MEJRA   It's normal to harm someone else?

STETKO   I've done nothing to you.

MEJRA   *(suddenly angry)* Pick up the rock.

STETKO   I can't.

               He grins.

               Funny thing about "dictators" eh?
               What happens when nobody does as they're told?
               What's the dictator to do? Kill them all?
               Then there'd be nobody left to do all the dirty work.
               Then the dictator isn't a dictator anymore.

Maybe everybody is pretending to be who they are. Maybe everybody has to believe a lie.

MEJRA   And what lie do you want to believe—that I'm here to save you, or to bury you alive?

STETKO   *(grins)* I believe you like me.
           But you're too old and ugly for a young guy like me.

MEJRA   Too ugly to be raped, too old to be impregnated. Just right for killing.

STETKO   For sure. We would have just shot you.

MEJRA   I would have considered myself lucky.

STETKO   Strange world, eh?

MEJRA   What will it be?
           Choose.

           Pause.

           Pick it up.

STETKO   No.

           Pause.

           MEJRA *starts digging* STETKO's *grave with her hands.*

           What are you doing?

MEJRA   Guess.

STETKO   You stupid bitch fucking cunt—

                He heaves the rock to his chest

MEJRA   *(slaps him across the face)* Don't ever call me that
                again.

STETKO   What's with you?
                I lift it.
                I drop it.
                Doesn't matter what I do I get slapped down.
                You wouldn't touch me if I wasn't tied up.

MEJRA   You wouldn't rape girls if they were armed.

STETKO   *(laughs)* Guess not.
                You think I'm stupid?
                I know they don't like it.

MEJRA   No they don't.

STETKO   You been raped?

MEJRA   None of your business.

STETKO   I take that for yes.

MEJRA   I don't care how you take it, just understand this,
                the military is not the only one with power.

STETKO   *(grins)* Untie me, Mejra.

MEJRA   *(grins back)* Not yet, Stinko.

STETKO   This rock is too fucking heavy.

MEJRA   Drop it—except on your foot—
             and I bury you alive.

STETKO   What is the point of this?

MEJRA   The right to choose.

STETKO   Hold it, break my foot, or be buried alive?!

MEJRA   I knew you had some potential, Stinko.

             She exits.

STETKO   Don't call me Stinko!
             It's Stetko.
             Stet-ko Tef-te-dar-i-ja.
             Stupid—

             *He stops short just in case she hears him. He
             holds the rock as the lights indicate the com-
             ing of night. He sings a marching tune, baldly,
             defiantly.*

             Blackout.

SCENE 4

             *MEJRA is bandaging STETKO's foot. He shivers
             from cold and shock.*

MEJRA   Papa cut his tail off and he howled and wailed
             through the night and in the morning the poison
             was out of his system.

The shock drove it out of his body.
He was my father's favorite dog.
He used to say "I loved that dog enough to chop its tail off—which is more than I could do for my children."

STETKO   What if he had died?

MEJRA   Who knows.
           We only ever know what does happen.

STETKO   I wouldn't have done that.
           I probably would have just watched, to see if he'd make it on his own.
           See if he was meant to live.

MEJRA   Who decides that?
           Who decides who will live and who won't?

STETKO   (shrugs) I don't know.

MEJRA   My father loved that dog.

STETKO   (grins) Like you love me?

MEJRA   I don't love you.

STETKO   You sure?

MEJRA   Positive.

STETKO   You live out here alone.
           No neighbours.
           Nothing.
           You see me. Young—

MEJRA   *(bursts out laughing)* You are so arrogant and stupid —
            I think all your brains must be in your cock.
            And you're impotent!

STETKO   Not anymore.
            Last night I had a hard on.
            That's why I dropped the rock.
            So I could masturbate.

MEJRA   You lie.

            Pause.

STETKO   Yeah.
            I couldn't hold it any longer.
            My back was killing me.
            In a way I was relieved when it fell.

MEJRA   Nothing like pain to stop… everything.

            I have something for you.

STETKO   A gift?

MEJRA   Sort of.
            I found it.

STETKO   What is it?

MEJRA   A rabbit.
            It had been caught in a snare and chewed its front
            paw off to escape.
            I was going to kill it for dinner but it snarled at me.
            I thought anything that wants to live that badly de-
            serves a chance. So I brought it home.

STETKO   I had a pet rabbit when I was seven.
          Where is it?

MEJRA   There, in the basket.

          STETKO limps to the basket, opens it, and looks in.

STETKO   It hissed at me!

MEJRA   Maybe it doesn't want our help.
          Maybe it wants to die.

STETKO   Nobody wants to die.

MEJRA   How do you know?

STETKO   ...I saw lots of people die.

MEJRA   The girls?

STETKO   Yeah. Some of them didn't seem to care.
          But they probably knew it was for the best. Nobody
          wants a woman who's been raped.
          Husbands walk away.

MEJRA   Mothers never walk away.

          Silence. STETKO considers this statement.

          That's where men always become confused.
          They don't know what to do about mothers.

STETKO   It bit me!

          He sucks his finger and closes the basket.

Look at me.
No ear.
Crushed foot.
Bit finger.

MEJRA   Should we kill it?

STETKO   —no.

MEJRA   Why not?

STETKO   It doesn't know any different.
           It doesn't know I'm a friend.

           What are you smiling about?

MEJRA   I'm not. I'm musing.
           We forgive an animal but not a people.

           Well, it's yours then.

           She gives him dinner.

           This is all there is.

STETKO   What is this?

MEJRA   It was growing near the marsh.

STETKO   A man can't live on this.

MEJRA   Eat the rabbit then. That's all there is.

           She exits.

STETKO   And what did you have, eh?!
            Beer?
            Potatoes with gravy?
            Some cabbage?
            Stewed beef and cabbage with potatoes and papri-
            ka, and carrots.
            Dumplings.
            I'll die on this!
            She's going to starve me to death.

            *The rabbit scratches at the basket. He opens it
            and looks in.*

            Where do you think you're going, eh? With three
            feet.
            What a pair.
            Maybe if we team up we'll have enough feet be-
            tween us to escape.

            Maybe I ought to eat you instead.
            Stay and eat—run and—
            and what?
            Be eaten?
            What a life, eh?
            Eat or be eaten.
            What a fucking life.
            That's it though, isn't it.
            At least for you.
            I'm a man.
            I'm supposed to be above that.

            (starting to eat) But I'm not.

            He shares some of his greens with the rabbit.

I'm not.

Blackout.

Scene 5

STETKO is bent over, looking closely at a small green growth in the plowed field. The rabbit is beside him in the basket. He straightens up suddenly and runs, still shackled, as far as the chain leash permits.

STETKO   MEJRAA!
Something is growing!

He runs back to the growth and examines it further.

A green thing.
What though?
It's not even in the row.
Maybe it's a weed.
(grins) Maybe it's—rabbit food!
That's what you wish, eh?
Is that what you wish?
A big green salad?
Even if it's a weed?
MEJRAAAA.

It must be a weed.
Nothing else is growing except it.
Do you like weeds, eh?
Would you like to try a leaf or two?

STETKO plucks a leaf but the whole plant comes up.

Oh shit! The whole thing's come up.
Maybe it was dying anyway.
What do you think?
A plant comes up that easy—can't be meant to live, eh?

He dangles it over the opened basket.

Feast your eyes on that.
Do you want it?
Roll over.
(laughs) You're no dummy.
Only dogs roll over for their dinner.
And play dead.
Because you're so smart you can have it.
Don't bite my fingers.
Gently.
You see, even a stupid animal can learn.
Yes, you'll let me pet you as long as I feed you.
It's nice, eh?
Feels good.

MEJRA enters with cut flowers.

MEJRA   Look what I found.
Growing.
Wildflowers.

STETKO   They're nice.
Pretty.

MEJRA   They're weeds really but who names the rose?

STETKO	Huh?
MEJRA	Never mind. Why were you shouting?
STETKO	Something was growing here too.
MEJRA	Of course. I planted it this morning. It's a wild-bean plant. I found it by the marsh. A lone survivor.
STETKO	Lone? The only one?
MEJRA	I don't know how it grew, but there it was, so I up- rooted it and brought it here.
STETKO	I don't think it will make it.
MEJRA	Why not?
STETKO	Too hot.
MEJRA	It's not too hot.
STETKO	Too dry.
MEJRA	We'll carry water from the mountains if we have to. It'll grow. It has to. That's all there is. What's the matter?

What have you done, Stinko?
You look—ridiculous.

She pushes him aside and can't see the plant.

Where is it!?

Did you eat it, you pig?!

STETKO   No.

MEJRA   Did you feed it to that damn rabbit!

STETKO   No.

MEJRA   Then where is it?

STETKO shrugs and looks confused.

Don't you realize that was our chance to grow
something?!

STETKO   I'll do without.

MEJRA   You idiot!
We'll all do without!

She sees the rabbit.

You fed it to the rabbit.
(snatching it) Give me that.

It is a gnawed nub.

Nothing.

Chewed the vital part first.

She strikes STETKO.

Shit for brains.

STETKO   I thought it was a weed.

MEJRA   It was!
           One we could eat.

STETKO   We'll find something else.

MEJRA   What?

STETKO   —Flowers.
           Mix them with something.
           Grass!
           Roast them.

MEJRA   I can't believe you!

STETKO   I didn't know!
           I wouldn't have done it if I'd known.
           Why didn't you tell me?

MEJRA   I don't have to report to you.

STETKO   No, but if you'd told me—if you'd said
           "Hey, Stinko, I planted a wild bean in the field,
           don't feed it to the rabbit—"

           *She realizes his attachment to the rabbit and
           makes a step toward it.*

MEJRA	Give me the rabbit.
STETKO	*(steps between it and her)* No.
MEJRA	Get out of my way.
STETKO	—No.
MEJRA	Move, or I'll beat you purple.
STETKO	Please, Mejra. She's mine.
MEJRA	She's not yours any more than the sun is yours. The air the water this land. You own nothing!
STETKO	Then why did you give her to me?
MEJRA	I heard something about your girlfriend. She was raped.
STETKO	You lie!
MEJRA	She was shot first. Killed. Then raped. She was lucky, wouldn't you say? She didn't have to endure the—what— indignity? Pain? A lucky girl.

STETKO	You lie.
MEJRA	Yes. I lie. We all lie. Why do we do that, Stetko? Why do you lie?
STETKO	I don't know.
MEJRA	Think!
STETKO	Depends on the lie.
MEJRA	You lied about the rabbit. You said she didn't eat the green. Why?
STETKO	I was afraid you'd hurt her.
MEJRA	Do you think the first lie ever told was to protect another?
STETKO	…Maybe.
MEJRA	You think we're that noble?
STETKO	Probably the first person to tell a lie did it to save himself.
MEJRA	From what? What are we saving ourselves from?
STETKO	I don't know.
MEJRA	Think!

What are you afraid of, Stetko?

Silence.

STETKO   What do you want to hear?
I'll say anything.
I don't care.
Whatever you want.
Do you think just because somebody says some-
thing they mean it?

MEJRA   You lie to make life easier for yourself?
It's more convenient to go along with the others?

STETKO   Sure.

MEJRA   You raped and killed girls because it was easier than
disobeying orders.

STETKO   Yes!
Yesyesyes!
It's easier to obey.
I obey authority.
I obey you.
It's easier.

MEJRA   I guess that's why the soldiers killed your girlfriend
first.
It's easier to rape them when they're dead.

STETKO   She wasn't raped!

MEJRA   Yes she was.
Gang raped.
From the back.

He covers his ears and sings, wildly fighting tears. MEJRA *exits.*

Lights indicate night and a lambent moon. STETKO *stops singing and sobs.*

Lights out.

SCENE 6

The same lambent moon. MEJRA *enters with a jar.* STETKO *stands defeated.*

MEJRA   I brought you a beer.

               He looks at it, at her, then takes it.

STETKO   *(ironic, toasting)* To life. *(and swallows a large mouthful)*
               It's warm.

MEJRA   Yes.

STETKO   Who cares, eh?
               To life!

               He drinks.

MEJRA   To life.
               To children.
               To love.

STETKO   To love.

Who knows about love?

MEJRA I do.

STETKO You are the cruellest woman I know.

MEJRA Kindness is not love.
Besides, I don't love you.

STETKO You hate me.

MEJRA Yes.

STETKO Why do you hate me so much?

    Silence.

Why did you bring me here?

MEJRA Drink up, Stetko.

STETKO Thank you.
For not calling me Stinko.

Is it late?

MEJRA Almost morning.

STETKO You couldn't sleep.

MEJRA No.

STETKO Me either.

MEJRA I know.

STETKO   You watch me?

MEJRA   I just know.

STETKO   Was she really raped?
          Tell me the truth, Mejra.

MEJRA   What is the truth?
          I tell you your girlfriend is dead.
          Raped.
          I can't show you the body.
          There is no body to be found.

          People tell you one thing.
          The military tells another.

          We'll read about the war in the papers — new territories divided among the victors.
          New leaders.
          Economic decisions determined by outside interests.
          There will be medals for the dead soldiers on all sides.
          Plaques for the brave and foolhardy.
          Monuments for the generals.

          What will anyone know about you and your girlfriend?
          About me?
          About the girls in the forest?

          What is the truth?

          The truth
          is like love.

It defies words.
It's known without "facts."

STETKO Was she or wasn't she?

MEJRA She's missing.
That's all we know.
That's the "facts."
Now, what is the truth?
You're a soldier. You know how a soldier's mind works.
Is she alive?
A virgin?

STETKO Maybe she's hiding.

MEJRA Yes, maybe she's hiding.

Silence.

STETKO Things happen in war.
We're trained to follow orders. Our lives depend on it. It's automatic.
Soldiers aren't supposed to think.
Only obey.

MEJRA I guess you'll bear the "other side" no ill will if they've captured your girlfriend.

STETKO *drinks.*

STETKO Warm beer is better than no beer.

MEJRA *(ironic)* "Facts" are better than truth.
Revenge is better than sorrow.

STETKO   I hope I never grow old and bitter like you.

MEJRA   Then chances are you'll die young.

STETKO   *(shrugs)* What can I do?
I'm a prisoner.
I do nothing.
I think nothing.

MEJRA   Right.
You're helpless.
I'm helpless.
We're all victims of fate.

She can see STETKO *thinking about the issue of fate.*

Is war fate?

STETKO   I don't know.

MEJRA   And the girls?

STETKO   *(shrugs)* A girl walks by
and—
In a war
you can get away with it.

Everybody's doing it.
Rape is just part of war.

That's how some men pump themselves up.
Get their adrenaline going.
Makes them reckless.
Fearless.

I've seen men run into the open afterwards, spray-
ing bullets.
Most of them get shot down, but some don't and
they come back looking like heroes.
Everyone cheers.
They get first pick of the women.

I never did it.
Run in the open.

MEJRA   You only shot women.

STETKO   Yeah.
That's how it was.

          He drinks.

          That was their fate.

MEJRA   They cut her tongue out
          and slit her open from her vagina to her navel
          and filled the hole with dirt
          and pissed on it.

STETKO   I don't believe you anymore.

MEJRA   That's right.
          We all know soldiers don't do that to women and
          children.
          Men don't do that sort of thing.
          We all know that.
          Isn't that the "truth"?

          Tomorrow we go to the forest.

She exits.

A pale light of dawn.

Blackout.

Scene 7

They stand in the forest.

STETKO   It's gone.

MEJRA   She.
She is not an it.

STETKO   She.
She's gone.
Animals must have got her.

MEJRA   This was the first one you killed?

STETKO   Yeah.

MEJRA   Where's the log? You said you put a log over her body.

STETKO   Someone must have taken it for firewood.

MEJRA   No evidence.

STETKO   No.

MEJRA   No one is going to know the truth.
That's the plan, isn't it?

Keep it secret.
No reminders.

Maybe you're lying.
Maybe this isn't the right place.

STETKO   This is the right place.

              Silence.

MEJRA   Do you know her name?

STETKO   I didn't ask.

MEJRA   Missing.
              That's her epitaph.
              Missing.

              Where are the others?

STETKO   I don't know.

MEJRA   You knew where she was, where are the others?

STETKO   I don't know.
              This was the first one I killed.
              The first always sticks in the mind.
              After that it was—
              I don't know—

MEJRA   Routine?

STETKO   Sort of.

MEJRA   What about the girl you liked the best?

The virgin.
What was her name?

STETKO   I don't know.

MEJRA   Think!

STETKO   I don't remember.

MEJRA   You don't remember or *won't* remember?

STETKO   I *don't* remember.

          Silence.

MEJRA   Where is she?

          Pause.

STETKO   A different place.

MEJRA   Where?

STETKO   In a grave.

MEJRA   You buried her?

STETKO   We dug a big grave and put lots of them in it.

MEJRA   Where is it?

STETKO   I don't remember!

MEJRA   Take me there.

STETKO   How can I when I don't know where it is?!

MEJRA   What will make you remember?

STETKO   What?

MEJRA   What do I have to do to you to make you remember?

STETKO   Some things are just gone from memory.
Blocked out.

MEJRA   *(hands him a shovel)* Start digging.

STETKO   It's not here!

MEJRA   Your own grave.
Start digging.

STETKO   Things have changed!
The markings are different.
Trees have been cut
and—

Looking up, remembering.

It was west,
the sun was in my eyes,
it was late afternoon.

MEJRA   Find it.

STETKO   There was a tree,
a large tree,
there were bullet holes in the bark
and a strong branch hung low—

the one I tied her up to.
I see it
but I don't know where it is now.

MEJRA   Then dig.

STETKO   I'm not sure where it is!

MEJRA   Then dig!

STETKO   Come on, Mejra.

MEJRA   *(strikes him)* Find her.

    Pause.

    STETKO wanders in one direction, stops, shakes his head, and then wanders in another direction.

STETKO   No.

    He wanders, thinks he's getting close, stops, uncertain. He takes a few steps farther. MEJRA stands impassive and watches.

    Meanwhile, the lighting has gradually changed to indicate the passing of time and a change of location. They are now deeper in the forest; it is darker, the shadows are longer.

    STETKO stops and looks down.

This is it.

    MEJRA comes to the spot.

MEJRA	Here?
STETKO	Yes.
MEJRA	Are you sure?
STETKO	I'm sure.
MEJRA	How do you know?
STETKO	I can tell. I can feel it.
MEJRA	Feel what?
STETKO	I don't know.

        STETKO *remembers.*

MEJRA	Tell me.

        Silence.

Tell me, Stetko.
They mustn't be forgotten.
Same as your girlfriend.
They must not be forgotten.

        Pause.

You liked her the best.

Tell me.

        Pause.

STETKO   I was driving the Jeep.
I was laughing.
Finally I was alone.
I got to drive on my own—with her,
this girl.
I felt really good.
The sun was shining the whole time.
I was singing,
I'm finally alone with this girl.
And I'm singing—

He sings a popular song.

I look over at her
and she's not smiling,
just looking straight ahead.
I'd forgot you see,
I forgot what I was supposed to be doing—
killing them.
I forgot.
I was suddenly a free man going for a ride with my
girl.

Then everything got serious.
I don't remember anything until we get here
and I tell her to lift her arms up over her head.
And she does.
I tie her hands together and throw the rope over the
tree branch.
It's gone now.
Somebody has cut it down.

I pull the rope till she's stretched as far as she can go
and then I pull till she's just off the ground.
She looks so pretty.

Big watery eyes
like a doe's.
I cut her dress—
because her hands are tied and I can't get it off
otherwise.
I use my hunting knife
She's got very white skin.
It's never seen the sun.
She's got a thin line of black hairs that run up to her
belly button.
I think it's quite sexy.
I tell her so.
I go up to her
and
put my arms around her
and kiss her neck.
I figure I can do it with her.
I feel her shiver.
I ask her if she's cold.
She says, "No."
I ask her if she's afraid.
She shakes her head
but I think she's lying.
I ask her if she wants me to undress—
maybe she hasn't seen a man before
naked.
She closes her eyes
tight.
So I tell her I won't take my clothes off
and she opens them again
and I can see she's crying.

So I stop
and sit down on a log
or rock

and I tell her about myself
and my uncle.
I tell her about my girlfriend.

I ask her what she wants to be when she grows up.
She says she wants to be a teacher.
I tell her she's just like my girlfriend,
wanting to put some good back into the world.
I tell her I would too
if I knew how.

I tell her she's beautiful.
I tell her I want to do it with her.

I figure maybe I can come with her.

She begs me not to
but I try anyway.

Only I can't.
I can't get hard.
It won't go in.
I can't do it anymore.

It's all over.

    Pause.

I don't know what to do.

She begs me to set her free.
And I'm thinking, "What if I do?"
What if I set her free. What will happen?
I'm scared—in case the others find out—
they'd kill me for letting the enemy go.

She says she won't tell anyone.
I notice her hands are swollen and white.
It's getting late,
the sun's going down,
I have to return the Jeep.

So I leave it to fate.
I say, "Let's see if she's meant to live."

I back away
and
close my eyes
and aim the gun
and I say to myself
if I miss,
no matter what,
I let her go.

> *Pause.*

It hit her in the face.

> *Silence.*

I cut her down and dragged her to a grave we'd dug
before but hadn't covered over
and I put her into it
and buried her.

> *Long, long silence.*

MEJRA   Dig it open.

STETKO   What!?

MEJRA   Dig the grave open.

STETKO   She's dead!

MEJRA   Dig it open!

STETKO   I can't.
               I'll be sick.

MEJRA   Be sick, but dig.

STETKO   What's the point!

MEJRA   Proof.

               We want the "facts."

STETKO   I did it like I said!

MEJRA   Stetko, you will dig open that grave or you will dig
               your own and lie in it.
               Choose.

                    Pause.

                    STETKO *takes the shovel and digs.*

STETKO   It's been a while.
               There might not be anything left.

MEJRA   Dig.

                    He digs.

STETKO   I hear corpses carry diseases.

MEJRA   None worse than any the living carry.

            He digs deeper.

STETKO   Maybe this is the wrong spot.

MEJRA   It'll be the right one for you.

            He digs even deeper.

STETKO   There were a lot of bodies.
            How will I know which is her?

MEJRA   Because her spirit will return and shriek her name.

            He drops the shovel and scrambles out. MEJRA
            blocks his way.

            Afraid of spirits?

STETKO   We shouldn't be doing this!

MEJRA   Why?
            Afraid to revisit?
            Do you feel graves are haunted—
            that the spirits of the dead linger on if their bodies
            have been brutalized?
            Murdered?

            Dig.

STETKO   It was a war!
            I only did as I was told!

MEJRA   Such a good boy.

What if you'd said no.

STETKO   They would have killed me.

MEJRA   Me or you.
It comes to that.
Me
or you.

STETKO   War changes everything.
Once you're in it—
there are no choices.

MEJRA   Yes there are.
Dig.

STETKO   Right.
"Dig."
Obey or die.
People will always obey rather than die.

MEJRA   Dig.

STETKO   Sure.
I'm not proud.
I'm no hero.
I'll dig.

He digs furiously.

I don't know about life.
I'm no great thinker.
What am I supposed to know that would change
things?

MEJRA   You should look at every woman as if she were your
         daughter.

              He stops.

         Every woman
         as if she were your daughter.

         Dig.

STETKO   I can't.

MEJRA   You can
         and you will.

STETKO   *(digs)* Okay.
         Big deal.
         Big f'ing deal.

         I've hit something.

MEJRA   Keep digging.

STETKO   I think *(looking closely, leaping out)* it's a head!

MEJRA   Pull it out.

              He looks frantic.

         Pull it out.

STETKO   I can't.

              Long silence.

STETKO walks into the grave and pulls at the corpse.

Okay!
It's out!

MEJRA   Bring her here.

STETKO   Oh God—

> *He hauls it up and tosses the small corpse at her feet.*

MEJRA   Who is she?

STETKO   I don't know.

MEJRA   What was her name?

STETKO   I don't know!

> *Pause.*

MEJRA   Dig up the rest.

STETKO   Oh god!
             Fucking hell—

> *He stomps into the grave and digs.*

> *MEJRA looks at the corpse and brushes dirt off the decomposing skull.*

MEJRA   How old, child?
             You will not be forgotten.

> STETKO *tosses another decomposed body on the ground.* MEJRA *goes to it and puts a finger through a hole in the breastbone.*

Was it quick
or did you suffocate in the grave?

> *Another body, and another are unceremoniously tossed out.* MEJRA *goes to one and bends low.*

Is it you?
(kneeling) Is it you?

> *She cradles the body in her arms, and rocks, and begins to keen.*

> STETKO *climbs out and observes. When* MEJRA *finally sees him she stops.*

> *A long, long silence.*

Come here.

> *He does.*

On your knees.

> *He hesitates but obeys.*

Hold her.

> *She offers the body to him.*

Hold her.

STETKO *reluctantly holds out his arms to receive the corpse.*

Her name is Ana.
She was nineteen.
Young looking for her age.
She wanted to be a teacher—of philosophy.
She respected all religions.
She was brave and kind at once.

She had a thin line of black hair that ran up to her navel.
And watery eyes
like a doe's.

She felt every person had dignity regardless of their race.

She believed love was the answer.
Patience was the teacher.
Compassion was the mirror.
She would say, "I am the reflection of love and trust and joy—all that you are
but haven't yet recognized
in yourself."

Silence.

I felt her adjust her shoulder before she entered this world. A world not yet ready for grace and beauty.

I never taught her about evil.
I thought I could protect her by hiding the truth.

Pause.

Give her back to me.

Pause.

STETKO *returns the corpse with as much grace and reverence as he can.* MEJRA *stands. Silence.*

You can get up now.

He doesn't.

No longer "missing."

Get up.

STETKO   I can't.

MEJRA   You are going to dig up the rest
and then you have one more task.

You are going to tell the story of the missing ones.
The women and children you killed.
You are going to name them.
We are going to build a monument to the truth
about war.
We are going to let the mothers reclaim their
daughters.

STETKO   They'll kill me.
Then the truth will never be out.

MEJRA   The truth has a way of emerging.
Nothing can stop it
once it's started.
I may be gagged,

my husband tortured,
my house burned down,
my land stolen,
my children savaged,
but the wind will speak my name,
the waters will tell the fish,
the fish will tell the hunter
"I am."
I am.

Blackout.

SCENE 8

*A monument of the dead bodies has been built.
The corpses have been seated, stacked in a circle,
looking out.*

*MEJRA is standing by the monument holding the
corpse of Ana in her arms. The basket with the
rabbit is near the monument. STETKO stands centre stage, holding one of the corpses in his arms.
He is uncertain and nervous.*

stetko   Uh…

            He looks at MEJRA.

MEJRA   Name them.

STETKO   I don't know who they are.

MEJRA   It's time.

STETKO	*(looking at the monument)* I don't know. It's a blur. You just did it.
MEJRA	"I." "I" did it.
STETKO	"I" just did it. I... killed them.

Silence.

My girlfriend is missing.
She has dark shoulder-length hair.
She wears it in a ponytail.

She has green eyes.
Her name
is Ini.
Ini Herak.

Pause.

MEJRA	Name all the girls you killed, Stetko.
STETKO	I didn't always ask their name.

Silence.

MEJRA	Describe them.
STETKO	I can't.

Pause.

MEJRA   Begin with the first.

STETKO   I don't know who she was.

MEJRA   What did she look like?

STETKO   …She was older.
               Maybe forty.

               After I shot her I hid her body under a log.

MEJRA   Remember her.

               He sets the corpse he is holding with the others.
               It triggers a memory.

STETKO   She had had children. I saw stretch marks on her
               belly.
               She had a birthmark near her left shoulder—a pur-
               ple one shaped like a kidney bean.

               Long silence.

               I killed a girl named Mini. Fifteen.
               She had a sunburned face.
               Luba, maybe twenty-one.
               And a young girl with reddish hair. Long. Down to
               her waist.
               A girl named Sara. She wore glasses. She was short
               and chubby.
               A married woman. She had a wedding ring with a
               tiny diamond set into the band.
               Monica. She had a gap between her two front teeth.

               A girl with one brown eye and one green one.

Carol. I think she was pregnant.

Eva. She was a swimmer in training for the Olympics.

A girl who said she was a waitress. She dyed her hair blond.

Dark roots were showing.

Misa. Sixteen.

Her older sister.

Twins. Thirteen. They looked identical.

A mother of two boys.

A girl with a scar on her right side.

An older woman who wore a copper bracelet on each wrist.

A girl with a mole beside her left nipple.

A girl with pimples.

A girl with black lace-up boots.

A girl with big soft lips.

He has trouble continuing.

Ana.

Ana.

MEJRA, *in a rage, rushes at* STETKO *with the shovel and strikes him on the back. He falls against the bodies and scrambles behind the monument.* MEJRA *pursues him and strikes him a single hard blow to the head. He falls still and silent, his feet extending beyond the bodies.*

Silence.

MEJRA *realizes she has killed him and is horrified. She fights back retching. She looks up and out and realizes her deed has been witnessed. She starts to flee, but can't. It's pointless. She's been seen and the deed too horrible to run from. She wants to scream but can't. She is like a caught animal. She runs back to* STETKO.

She decides to bury him, and after glancing around for a suitable spot, proceeds to drag him out by his feet. She begins to dig a hole when STETKO *groans. She hears him and rushes to him, grabbing his head in her hands.*

MEJRA   Stetko?
          Stetko!
          Are you—?!

          She checks his breathing and unconsciously, ec-static, hugs him to her chest.

          STETKO *stirs.* MEJRA, *aware of her compromise, abruptly drops his head, stands up, apart, and resumes a hardness.* STETKO *sits up and rubs his head.*

          Silence.

STETKO   So, you're glad I'm alive, eh?

          You're just like me, Mejra.
          A murderer.
          A slave and a dog.

MEJRA   Don't you compare us!

STETKO   "If you hate enough you can kill a people on command?"
          Who commanded you?

You think you're above it all, eh?
Once you got what you wanted from me then you
were going to do me in. Just like we do to prisoners.
You'd make a good soldier, Mejra.

MEJRA   I did it for my daughter!

STETKO   I had no daughter.
Only me.
Who are you to say who's more important?

MEJRA   I was doing it for love.

STETKO   That's what the soldiers say.
"Love for my country."

MEJRA   It's not the same!

STETKO   We all have our reasons, eh?
We all think we're right.

So, what's the answer,
eh, Mejra?

MEJRA   She was innocent!

STETKO   War is no place for the innocent.

MEJRA   How dare you!

STETKO   Going to kill me again?

MEJRA *stops.*

Silence.

Me or you.
Isn't that what you said?
Me
or you.

Who's it going to be?

Why don't you look at every man as if he were your son?

    Silence.

MEJRA   Would you have died to save your girlfriend?

STETKO   I don't know.
How do we ever know that?

MEJRA   I would have cut my own throat to save Ana.
I would have endured rape by every last soldier.
They could have flayed me alive and dragged my wet body through the streets.

STETKO   And you would kill for her too.

You can't win a war by dying for the enemy.

    Pause.

You willing to die for me, Mejra?

    She is outraged at the idea. STETKO *laughs at her.*

So much for ideals, eh?

It's easy to hate.

Easy to kill once you feed that hate.

Isn't that right, Mejra?

MEJRA   You make life unendurable.

STETKO   But we're here.
You're here.
I'm here.
We made it.

MEJRA   Yes.
There's no justice in this world.

STETKO   No.
Dogs and slaves.

MEJRA   Dogs and slaves.

> *Long silence.*

Get out of here.

> *She tosses him the keys to his chains.*

You're free to go.

> STETKO *does not go.*

Go.

> MEJRA *turns to leave.*

STETKO   Where will you go?

MEJRA	Back to the land.
STETKO	Can I go with you?
MEJRA	No.
STETKO	You need someone.
MEJRA	Not you.
STETKO	Who then?
	There is no one, is there? You're alone.
MEJRA	Go home to your family.
STETKO	They might take me back.
MEJRA	So go.
STETKO	Mejra?

No response.

I'm sorry.
I'm sorry for what I did.

Pause.

Forgive me.

MEJRA	How?
STETKO	Pardon?

MEJRA   How can I forgive you?
Show me.
Show me how to forgive.
I don't know how.

STETKO takes an uncertain step toward MEJRA.

STETKO   *(almost a whisper)* I'm sorry.

He unconsciously reaches out a finger to touch MEJRA's hand.

Forgive me.

MEJRA unconsciously makes a movement in his direction.

Slow fade on the monument of MEJRA and STETKO in a moment of possibilities.

The End.

Acknowledgements

There have been so many people who supported this project. Many have already been thanked, but I wish to make special mention of the following: Iris Turcott and Candace Burley for nurturing this play from its first thirty pages; Don Kugler and Richard Rose for believing in me for all those years, and for having the courage to produce the play; Rosemary Dunsmore and Peter Van Wart for their exceptional help and friendship; Dave Woolacott, who has supported and encouraged me through many creative projects and to whom I owe a special thanks; Jane Longo and Dianna Last, who gave me a space to write and unconditional love.

I also want to acknowledge and thank the Canada Council, the Ontario Arts Council, the Banff Playwrights Colony, the New Play Development Centre at Canadian Stage Company, Necessary Angel Theatre, and Northern Light Theatre for their assistance in the development of the play.

Colleen Wagner was born in Alberta and studied at the Ontario College of Art and at the University of Toronto. Her writing includes screenplays, stage plays, poetry, and short fiction. Her first play, *Sand*, was shortlisted for best international play at the Royal Exchange Theatre in Manchester, England. Other plays include Governor General's Literary Award–winner *The Monument*, which has been translated into a dozen languages and continues to be produced internationally; *The Morning Bird* (published by Scirocco Drama); *down from heaven* (nominated for a MECCA award for best new play); and *Home* (published by Scirocco Drama). Her recent documentary play *The Living*, based on stories of survivors in post-conflict zones, premiered at the SummerWorks Performance Festival in 2015 and won the NOW Audience Choice Award and will be published by TalonBooks in spring 2019. She co-founded and was co-artistic director of The NotaBle Acts Theatre Company in Fredericton, NB, from 2002 to 2007. She divides her time between a riverside farm in New Brunswick and downtown Toronto and teaches at York University. Visit www.colleenwagner.ca for more information.

Second edition: September 2010
Third printing: July 2018
Printed and bound in Canada by Imprimerie Gauvin, Gatineau

Cover photo by Cylla von Tiedemann
Cover and type design by Blake Sproule

**PLAYWRIGHTS
CANADA PRESS**

202-269 Richmond St. W.
Toronto, ON
M5V 1X1

416.703.0013
info@playwrightscanada.com
playwrightscanada.com